Outcast

Outcast

NO ROOM AT THE TABLE
FOR CONSERVATIVE BLACKS
IN BLACK AMERICA

• • •

Claston A. Bernard

ISBN-13: 9781983573774
ISBN-10: 1983573779
Library of Congress Control Number: 2018900370
CreateSpace Independent Publishing Platform
North Charleston, South Carolina

Contents

To Quantez, my beautiful wife, and my beautiful family. Thank you for allowing me the time to put my thoughts together. To my parents, Claston E. and Florence Bernard, thanks for your sacrifices. I love you guys. Sisters and brother, much love.

Preface
The Message

● ● ●

"He created them male and female and blessed them. And he named them 'mankind' when they were created" (Gen. 5:2 NIV).

"We hold these truths to be self-evident, that all men are created equal, that they are endowed by their Creator with certain unalienable rights, that among these are life, liberty, and the pursuit of happiness" (the US Declaration of Independence).

Those are messages showing that our rights should not be infringed upon by anyone or any government, irrespective of how one looks. Our color is immutable and sacred and should be treated as such. Any laws passed restricting those rights are illegal and a perversion of justice.

Some of us believe that God is the ultimate Creator who created us with unalienable rights, so why do we continue to allow some hatred or evil dictate how we live our lives? For example, you say some people are racist, and they will not treat me fairly or with respect. Why do they instantly assume the inferior position? Even if all that is true, why not create and then follow your path to economic success?

Should black Americans continue to believe that government is the cure for their every condition? If they do, they will continue to be used by the many deceptive leftist politicians and race hustlers seeking power while feeding them hatred for the white man. To liberate yourself from such bondage, you have to look within, be disciplined, and work hard. Blacks have become pawns in the left's move to socialize the American government, and if that happens, they will suffer en masse.

I have come to the point in my life where my worldview has changed. I had to move on. In this book I will explore what I believe to be some of the reasons that most conservative values are marginalized and even flatly rejected by the Democratic Party. There are instances in which Republicans have used prejudices against blacks. I am not excusing those behaviors, which I will talk about later. However, the majority in the Democratic Party seem to make prejudice, identity politics, groupthink, and socialist ideologies their primary platform. Those, I believe, do more harm to the black race. We do not need such labels.

Conservatives believe in God-given rights, limited government, and individual responsibilities. For me, it has been a long walk to that point, but my beliefs about family, education, and less governance eventually drove me to embrace my deeply held conservative views. I believe conservatives have an excellent platform. However, if they want to win more blacks to the conservative platform, they will need to fix how they handle messages on perceived racial matters, not platform.

There is a culture shift in America, one that seeks to silence conservative voices, debase the sacred, and introduce quasi-history as facts. That creates a longing to erase the past with the intent of erasing hurt or what has been viewed as criminal wrongs. However, erasing past hurts cannot fix the current black condition.

Postmodernism has become the order of the day, and many educated blacks have embraced that ideology because they believe it will liberate them from the white man's religion, only to realize that baskets are not designed to carry water. Views without anchors lead to destruction. If the black community wants to save itself, it will have to go back to an anchor that is immovable. And that is the truth.

History is there for us to learn from so as not to repeat mistakes. Having sympathy for those incidents of the past (slavery and Jim Crow) is OK. However, when we attempt to interject ourselves into an era that no longer exists, we tend to view things as we see them in our current culture. In black America, slavery and Jim Crow have left an ugly stain on this country's rich history. Irrespective of that stain, blacks have risen to every lofty level of power and success that this world has to offer. But even with those achievements, outside forces, slavery, and racism are regularly blamed for the ills of black America.

We do know that evil and hatred exist; we also know that there are still some Americans with strong racial prejudices (some groups already identify themselves). But when well-meaning Americans are called racist Uncle Toms for speaking the truth or standing for it, how do you convince black Americans to move beyond their victimization and start looking at things from a rational perspective and not an emotional standpoint?

Black culture and American culture are incompatible—you are either an American willing to live by American ideals and abide by the US Constitution, or you continue to fight to maintain the illusion of a separate culture, too afraid to assimilate. The truth is no respecter of persons or emotions. It is time we start embracing the reality of what kind of country America is.

In today's black American culture there seems to be a belief that government can fix all of black America's problems, the idea that through new laws and legislation the state can right the wrongs of slavery and Jim Crow and level the playing fields to economic prosperity. However, that kind of thinking is why I believe so many blacks have surrendered their rights. They think more laws and social programs will help them become a more prosperous group. The Democratic Party has used the injuries of slavery and Jim Crow to cause mass hysteria within the black community.

Racial-identity politics has created the illusion of fighting for the same causes and projects, the perception of so much unity among the churches, the entertainment industry, and the politicians who believe they speak for all minorities.

That type of behavior by Democrats is a play out of the Marxist/socialist playbook. Marxism believes that private ownership of property should be abolished, and the means of production should be owned by all citizens. Socialism concentrates the power of a nation in the hands of a few who dictate to the masses. Those systems promise material success and equality in which man is the measure of all things equal, and the government is the god that can fix your every problem. I believe that the more you understand the workings of the Democratic Party, the more you will move away from such deception because the truth will liberate you from the chains of lies.

Many blacks have fought to end identity associations. However, blacks are automatically assumed to be Democrats. That does hold true politically for the most part as voting history rightly shows. In fact, as of today 87 percent of blacks consider themselves Democrats with only 7 percent indentifying as Republicans.

The reality, according to Blackdemographics.com, is that less than 30 percent of blacks consider themselves liberals, and more than 40 percent consider themselves moderates. If the above numbers are correct, then why have blacks voted for Democrats at about a sixty-five percent rate or higher in just about every presidential election since the 1930s and above 90 percent in the past decade or two?

Blacks also are assumed to have each other's backs by simply being black, irrespective of one's moral leanings. Furthermore, blacks are expected to support every cause of black culture as long it is being led by someone black, or so it seems. How can you advocate ending identity politics when it is so ingrained in everyday black life? If you believe your color makes you superior, that is your right; just remember that other people have the same right and should not be categorized as being hateful or bigoted for preferring their race—unless being into color means something else to you, and you are too afraid to say what that is, so that is then projected onto other groups.

According to the National Human Genome Research Institute, Humans are 99.9 percent of the same genetic makeup, irrespective of color. Race in modern culture came about a few hundred years ago when some whites wanted blacks to think whites were superior; however, that was pseudoscience. Unfortunately, that kind of thinking has led to race becoming a political weapon used primarily by those on the left.

First, the Democratic Party used race to institute Jim Crow in the belief that whites were racially superior. Now the party is using race to control blacks by dividing America. The policy that seems to matter the most to many black Americans when it comes to politics is color. The Democrats, being well aware of that, take full advantage: vote color, not policy. That, I believe, is not a path to progress or to ending intergenerational poverty. If we were to live our lives as one America, we would still be able to live as individuals while achieving much success.

I believe that the condition of blacks suffering today is mainly due to the support of bad political candidates and weak family structure, and those factors lead to mental anguish and resentment, causes those on the left are too willing to exploit. (I will address an example of that situation in chapter one.) The left has unwittingly used blacks by fueling their anger to attack symbols of America's history and will stop at nothing to see their socialistic agendas fulfilled.

Another one of the left's ploys is to attack capitalism using various socialist arguments. But like science, capitalism is not about feelings; it is a system designed to allow and elevate individuals to control their destinies. If liberals would leave blacks alone, we could do much better by ourselves. Unshackle us from your doctrines; we do not need your pity or spokespersons.

If someone refuses to serve you, take your business elsewhere and that business will suffer. A company or person should not be forced by the government to serve anyone. People should have the right to refuse services to you if you impose on their rights and beliefs as long as they do not infringe on your natural rights; it is their right to do that. By the creation of superficial rights and cumbersome legislation, people with sincerely held beliefs—or those driven merely by their hatred—are at the mercy of the government. I believe any laws that infringe on life, liberty, property, and individuality are superficial; laws are supposed to protect those rights. For instance, forcing baker Jack Phillips of Colorado to bake a cake for a same-sex wedding is a violation of religious liberty and free speech protected by the First Amendment. This is not an argument endorsing any forms of discrimination. It is part of living in a free society. Such people should have a right to disagree and live out their beliefs.

In a culture supposedly dependent on God and the church, distinguishing among the church, the entertainment industry, and political culture seems almost impossible. The same faces that are seen in the popular cultures of politics and entertainment seem to dominate the church. In my experience, there are some black Christians who are sincere in their practices and have a genuine care for their fellow humans. However, the moment I differ politically from their views, then I am looked at as weird, an Uncle Tom, or one who has been brainwashed by the white man.

Many blacks claim to be Christians but support the Democratic Party, a party that has been taken over by the most intolerant liberals/leftists who push policies or ideologies that contradict biblical teachings.

Some families have voted democratically historically. But now they have a family member who supports the Republican Party, and that family member is treated with revulsion implicitly and, sometimes, explicitly. What is causing those reactions?

We are also able to protect ourselves and use the legal system the same as anyone, even though that is not a popular narrative today. Although due process can be hampered due to lack of funds, it should be pointed out that all citizens have a right to a speedy and public trial as guaranteed by the Sixth Amendment. As a Christian, I believe that God gave us the right to protect ourselves, and until hatred manifests itself in the physical, trying to change evil in a man's heart is as fleeting as chasing the wind. We know we cannot change the heart through laws or legislation—only God can do that—but our society provides us with enough protection against evil.

Unlike the past when legal barriers restricted the free movement of many blacks and their fundamental rights, that is not the case today. Even then legal restrictions were unable to stop black success in the cases of Frederick Douglas, Booker T. Washington, Carter G. Woodson, and George Washington Carver, to name a few. Today, blacks have done exceedingly well for themselves.

A political or economic system does not dictate our right to be human. Our Creator (triune God) created us. Every system that has been built should be established to serve the purpose of the human family. Within this human family there is no superior race, only male and female. The white man, by his conquest and expansion into the Americas—the West—was not made morally, economically, or physically superior to all other races; it is self-defeating to think that way. By contrast, I believe that most whites in modern American culture have an interest in success for all. Lack of success takes away from their accomplishments and family stability. One should find it hard to believe that most whites in today's culture sit around trying to see how they can keep the black man down; they, themselves, have problems too, and some also suffer from broken families. Most people, I would assume, are too consumed with themselves to be thinking about others; one only has to look at social media.

This book does not focus on those who hold irrational views through hatred of blacks. Instead, this book is for blacks and whites who see the destruction of the American family—black families and some white families—black culture, and American culture. It is for people who want to speak out about these self-defeating cycles and who want blacks to liberate themselves from impoverished minds, family destruction, and media indoctrination. I believe that until black American culture merges with mainstream American culture so that blacks identify with being American first, that destruction will be harder to stop.

To be truly American is to understand the past, live in the present, and embrace the future when it comes. When we compartmentalize evil and attribute it only to other groups, we tend to miss the evil within us. We all could self-examine and realize that we are all different in some ways (0.01 percent) but belong to the same human family (99.9 percent). Remember: the paint does not make a house; it merely adds sheen and beauty to it. We have far more differences in ideology than in biology.

Some will say and do mean and hateful things to others, but because speech does not fit the context of what popular narratives consider hate speech, we believe we get a free pass to attack with venom people who look like us even though Hitler could not dream of such a thing. For instance, how is calling another black man "Uncle Tom" any different from a white man calling a black man "nigger"? The spirit that drives a black man to call another black man "Uncle Tom" is the same spirit operating when a white man uses the term to insult a black man, and that spirit is evil.

Understandably, using racial slurs to describe any group is insensitive and downright hateful and should not be condoned. However, we cannot try to lump and dissect everything someone says because we dislike that person and think of him or her as being racist. Most times the cold, hard truth is brutal, and it is one of the reasons the republic has protected free speech.

No one has influenced me to believe these things; it took time and care to search out the facts and come to the understanding that I have today. I believe in family values and political freedom. The way forward is through individual business successes that should not be shackled by government overreach, overregulation, or high taxes.

People will undoubtedly ask what makes me an expert in this field, and my answer is this: I hunger for truth. While I was at Louisiana State University, because I love history, I enrolled in three history courses: Intro to Western Civilization, Black American History, and the Civil Rights Movement, although I majored in human resource management. Even though I did not pursue a minor in history, I continued to acquire books on history, especially black American history and the history of Western civilization.

My entry into politics in 2012 further bolstered my efforts to learn more about how black American history and Western civilization intersected and how those two histories have shaped the way of life for many Americans. I believe that black American history is part of the history of Western civilization and is a great American history. Studying both will help lead you to an understanding of the current state of the American political climate.

CHAPTER 1

Black Culture and Politics

● ● ●

"You are not one of us." "You are not from here." "You do not understand." "Why don't you go back where you came from?" "You are an Uncle Tom." "You are brainwashed." "You are a sellout." Those are the words that were spoken by one black man to another. It does not matter that an innocent black man was just gunned down by a fellow black, and that heinous act repulses you; however, you should not say anything that appears to be critical of the behavior of fellow blacks. After all, that response is a product of the past disenfranchisement of blacks. The system is to be blamed for such actions.

It would seem that within most areas of black culture, all harmful behaviors should be tolerated and accepted as products of outside oppression. I do not believe this to be the case. But for some reason, it appears that most blacks have been taught that to speak up against evil within their own community is a bad thing. But the reality is that someone innocent is now dead. America is black America's country. Irrespective of what others may say, blacks should understand that what happens in the black community is an American problem. All well-meaning Americans should be concerned.

When blacks like me speak out about the issues mentioned earlier, it is said that we listen only to conservative networks while being called other names. Some people would go further and say we have been brainwashed by white conservatives even though we arrived at our observations on our own or by doing research. It would seem that truth does not matter to such accusers. If it did, they would come to the understanding that truth is objective, so it does not matter where it originates.

You decide to watch television for some entertainment. There on the screen a famous gospel artist is onstage with the most secular of artists performing. It is not simply the act of being in the same place with the artist, but this particular artist holds some of the most hostile views of God and the family. Let me be clear: I believe there is nothing wrong with being onstage with good musicians whose music is their gift from God. However, when individuals make it their business to debase the sacred, gospel artists should not be associated with that.

Further, the pastor with the mega following appears to be continually courting those in popular entertainment for more visibility, a more significant audience, and financial success. When you question such behaviors, you are called judgmental and branded a hater.

While watching a political commentary you notice that educated blacks who have distinguished themselves in academia, the arts, economics, and politics but have conservative values are vilified and called all types of derogatory names. How can that be? How can you ask children to be the best but then, when they become adults and achieve lofty successes, regard them as fools because they do not embrace the majority black ideology that says, "We are all in this together"?

I have yet to see many notable A-list black celebrities or black leaders in modern times come to the support of conservative Republican values that are deemed by liberals as controversial but that are detrimental to the black community. For instance, liberals believe welfare is necessary to level the playing field, and so it must be protected. However, conservatives believe long-term welfare cripples a community or groups and want people to be more self-reliant. Some seem deeply afraid of being labeled as sellouts—or even worse—so they stay in the shadows. The ones who speak up are vilified.

A favorite argument is that until the Republican Party does more for the black community or changes its approach to black causes, that will not change. I agree that there are cultural misunderstandings between blacks and whites, but cultural ignorance does not equal racial prejudice. I do believe that more can always be done to help the least fortunate among us. I dare say that this has been done already. It is for us to see this and use the vast economic opportunities of America to enrich ourselves while using the political process to protect life, liberty, individuality, and property.

As I will demonstrate below, what blacks have been unwittingly caught up in is a political fistfight that will use their most vulnerable emotions to control them. This is the ideology of today's Democrats—identity politics—and it has been exceedingly detrimental to the black community.

How is it that political candidates, white or black, who support killing babies at any stage of pregnancy, who support gay marriage, and whose party values are hostile to God can walk into a black church and find significant black support? When does color come before God and family values? I can hear the objections that the whites are racist—especially those in the Republican Party—so blacks have no other choice. But to vote Democrat the questions are these: How are Republicans racist toward blacks, and has that alleged racism prevented blacks from achieving major success? Who sets the standard for racism?

How Did We Get Here?

After the Europeans' discovery of the Americas they established plantations in the new territories; those estates needed new labor because the indigenous peoples were not strong enough to handle the harsh labor conditions on plantations and the diseases brought by the Europeans.

The Europeans then turned to the Arabs for supplies, and the Arabs went to Africa and provided the Europeans with labor from the African West Coast. Eventually, the demand for slave labor grew so that major European powers sent ships to Africa to fill the high demand. Slavery had been a part of the old world and continued with the Europeans' expansion into the Americas. Finally, after more than 200 years, the United States of America declared independence from England.

The focus of this book is primarily on blacks in America. In the early formation of our country many, especially in the Southern States, supported the evil institution of slavery. The system of slavery in itself was an illegal act and was an encroachment on the liberties of Africans who found themselves as slaves on American plantations.

The unfortunate system of slavery received strong support from many US officials. That assault on human liberty was in stark contrast to the laws of God (natural rights) and the preamble to the US Constitution which declares, "We the people of the United States, in order to form a more perfect union, establish justice, insure domestic tranquility, provide for the common defense, promote the general welfare, and secure the blessings of liberty to ourselves and our posterity, do ordain and establish this Constitution for the United States of America." Furthermore, the US Declaration of Independence recognized that "all men are created equal," a direct contradiction of slavery.

The framers of the Declaration of Independence, some of whom owned slaves, knew that to obtain the support of the thirteen colonies for independence from England there would have to be compromises. Slavery was an illegal economic system, but it was the backbone of most Southern States.

At the US Constitutional Convention in 1787 a compromise was forged between the Northern and Southern States about how taxes would be paid based on population. Slaves could not vote, but slave states wanted the slaves counted for voting purposes. Doing so allowed whites from the Southern States to control the Electoral College and, thus, the presidential election process. The proposal for taxation was that states with slaves would pay taxes based on their population, their slaves, and their wealth. Those without slaves would be taxed based on their population and wealth. Three-fifths of slaves population counted toward voting.

As slaves were property, that three-fifths compromise gave the Southern States power and a more significant share of delegates in the House of Representatives. When the new Democratic Party was formed in 1828 it solidified control of the electorate to the Democrats, and it was a proslavery party. In fact, slavery would not have expanded into other territories without that compromise.

In 1857 the US Supreme Court ruled against Dred Scott, a former slave who had moved from a slave state, Missouri, to a free state, Wisconsin. While living in Wisconsin, Scott petitioned the courts for his freedom.

However, the US Supreme Court ruled that a slave could not be afforded freedom because slaves were not considered citizens of the United States.

That three-fifths compromise did not change until after the Civil War when the Thirteenth Amendment made slavery illegal in 1865 and when the Fourteenth Amendment—passed in 1868 by a Republican Congress— counted slaves as whole persons, granting them citizenship and abolishing the practice of considering slaves as property.

The inhumane treatment that was meted out to the slaves was terrible and against natural laws. However, in the writing of that great document called the US Constitution, the pieces were installed that eventually led to the institution of slavery coming down. Many Americans knew back then that if slavery were not ended, it would eventually destroy the Union because slavery violated the laws of liberty.

In 1854 a new political party, the Republicans, was formed with the intention of abolishing slavery. President Abraham Lincoln was the party leader. After the death of more than 700,000 enslaved souls, the evil institution of slavery was defeated. That ushered in a new period in the lives of former slaves who were finally able to move about freely and participate in political life.

The Thirteenth, Fourteenth, and Fifteenth Amendments gave blacks many rights that they exercised generously. The period following the abolition of slavery is popularly referred to as Reconstruction when former slaves were elected to political office and also enjoyed business success.

The combination of black and Republican voters made the ex-slaves a political force. The Democratic Party, wanting to break that Republican stronghold, supported the formation of the KKK in 1864 and the White League in the 1870s. Those local radical groups started terrorizing blacks and Republicans. They drove fear into blacks and Republicans with their killings and beatings, causing many to flee. The Democratic Party, through those terrorist groups, was able to gain control of the Southern political climate. Racial policies, namely Jim Crow, were introduced during a period when the legal system discriminated against blacks.

Democratic legislators introduced the black code in 1865 to disenfranchise blacks; those laws also were used to restrict the free movement of blacks. One incident I would like to refer to was the expulsion of twenty-nine black legislators by Democrats, and some Republicans, in Georgia. Mr. Henry Turner McNeal, one of the ousted black legislators, placed the blame squarely on the Democrats and called the Democratic Party an enemy of the black man.

The 1876 presidential campaign saw the election of Rutherford B. Hayes, a Republican. His election eventually brought about a secret compromise that resulted in the federal government leaving the South. That federal pullout officially ended Reconstruction, and the resulting vacuum left the South at the mercy of the Democratic Party.

By the early 1890s the Democrats had removed the Republican Party from most Southern States. For blacks to vote, they had to pay poll taxes, pass literacy tests, and meet residency requirements. If you were black in some areas of some states, you could not vote. The South became a one-party region—a Democratic Party stronghold.

Conditions in the Southern States continually worsened for blacks during that period, and they were dealt another major blow in 1896 with *Plessy v. Ferguson*. Homer Plessy, a light-skinned black man from New Orleans, had purchased a ticket to travel on a train with whites; authorities arrested him for breaking the law.

Plessy sued, using the argument that under the Fourteenth Amendment he was guaranteed equal protection. The case went to the Supreme Court, which ruled against Plessy, claiming that segregation did not make him inferior or deprive him of his rights. The majority of justices on the Supreme Court argued that states could establish separate but equal facilities, and in a political system such as the Democratic South, whites enjoyed the superior facilities, entirely segregating the public sphere. That was a terrible decision by the Supreme Court—a case of judicial activism, which is deciding cases based on preferences rather than applying the rule of law. That decision gave Jim Crow teeth and inflicted untold injuries on black Americans.

The Constitution, as created by the founders, gave the legislative branch (Congress) the power to make laws. Congress consists of the house and senate. The members of the house and senate are elected by the people from each state. The executive branch, which is the office of the president, has the power to enforce the laws. The judicial power, led by the Supreme Court, interprets the laws and decides the facts.

The federal courts have given the federal government power to legislate issues that were not their responsibilities. Sadly, the courts often misinterpreted the laws and, as in the Plessy ruling, took away the constitutional rights of blacks. That Plessy decision is an example of what happens when laws are not used for their designed purposes; it is a perversion of justice. Those Supreme Court justices were partisan and were influenced by popular sentiment rather than sticking to the facts.

The election of Democrat Woodrow Wilson as president in 1912 saw the segregation of the federal government. Wilson promised blacks that, if they voted for him, he would help their causes, and he wanted blacks to advance the interests of their race. However, shortly after he took office, his cabinet members began the process of segregating the federal government, mainly the US Treasury and the US Postal Service.

The New Deal in the 1930s and 1940s under President Franklin D. Roosevelt, a Democrat, provided limited support to blacks but generous support to whites, and it created significant shifts in the political process. Blacks left the Republican Party and started voting mainly for Democrats. A significant number of blacks have supported the Democratic Party ever since.

The Republicans attempted to introduce desegregation laws in the 1940s, but those attempts failed. But desegregation received a boost with the election of President Dwight D. Eisenhower, a Republican, in 1950. Under his watch, the Supreme Court ruled in *Brown v. Board of Education* for desegregation of the public education system, and federal troops were ordered to the South to ensure that the schools were desegregated. That marked the first time federal troops were back in the South since their 1876 pullout during Reconstruction. In 1957, again under Eisenhower, the Civil Rights Act paved the way for the final passage of the 1964 Civil Rights and Voting Rights Acts.

The Civil Rights Act of 1964 banned discrimination based on race, color, sex, religion, and national origin. The 1965 Voting Rights Act guaranteed that racial minorities could vote, and it abolished the literacy voting test. It has long been believed that the majority of blacks shifted their support to the Democratic Party during the '60s after passage of the Civil Rights and Voting Rights Acts because the Democrats were the ones who guaranteed passage, but the facts do not support that belief. The shift happened much earlier, in the late 1930s during the New Deal at the peak of racial discrimination.

The Civil Rights Bill received majority support from the Republicans in Congress and was signed into law by Democratic President Lyndon B. Johnson. Johnson fought for most of his political life against desegregation. He was also known for his racial comments toward blacks, supposedly referring to bills that benefited blacks as "nigger bills." It is alleged that before he signed the Civil Right Acts he said, "I will have niggers voting for Democrats for the next 200 years."

Now I will say there are not many sources to verify that comment, though Johnson never denied saying it. Sadly, if true, more than fifty years later, the majority of blacks are still supporting the Democratic Party. You do not have to take my word for it; the history is there to be researched to see the kind of man President Johnson, the supposed civil rights icon, really was to black people.

Johnson's opponent in the 1964 presidential election, Republican Senator Barry Goldwater, appealed for votes from Southern Democrats who were opposed to the Civil Rights Act. Because of that move by Goldwater, Republicans have been blamed for not passing the bill and have struggled to gain 15 percent of black votes in every presidential election since. The signing of the legislation by Johnson was a political move to increase power by solidifying the black vote for the Democratic Party.

However, this is not the popular narrative. It is said that the passage of the Civil Rights Act caused the majority of racist whites to leave the Democratic Party and start voting Republican; however, the numbers do not indicate that. As stated earlier, the shift by blacks began heavily in the 1930s. Southern racists voted overwhelmingly for Franklin D. Roosevelt, who gave some benefits to blacks in the Jim Crow era, but that did not cause the racists to leave the party. So what incentives would Democrats have to leave the party after the civil rights bills passed in 1964?

I believe a more honest narrative is that some Republicans did use racial prejudices to their advantage as Barry Goldwater did in appealing to southern Democrats, but they paid dearly. Others stood aside and allowed Democrats to push bills that were detrimental to blacks, like I stated in the preface. However, that is not the Republican platform, and a majority of Republican policies do not indicate racial prejudice.

My attraction to the Republican Party is to the policies that support upward progress, social conservatism, individuality, and national pride. The Republican Party started dominating Southern politics in the 1980s, well after the Civil Rights bill of 1964. Simply put, the Republican Party platform is the platform for hardworking, middle-class Americans. That stands in stark contrast to the socialistic agenda of state control and broad regulations of Democratic Party policies.

It is said the Republicans use coded terms to turn out racists, but I have yet to see those coded racial policies. It is my understanding that the coding issues have to do with abolishing affirmative action or welfare for single mothers. Take welfare for single mothers: both blacks and whites are beneficiaries, with a more significant number of whites receiving assistance, so how can you argue that wanting this program abolished suggests racial prejudice? I am opposed to affirmative action: does that make me racist?

People will undoubtedly point out that many blacks have left the Southern states due to racial prejudices. That trend is reversing as many families that fled during the Jim Crow era have been returning southward, fleeing high taxes and big-city government for the friendlier South. Once you leave the Bronx and Brooklyn, for example, you do not have to look hard to see the effects of Democratic policies on racial disparities as you head toward Manhattan. The Republican Party was formed to end slavery and the kind of gap that keeps people on minimum wage with their hands out to the government.

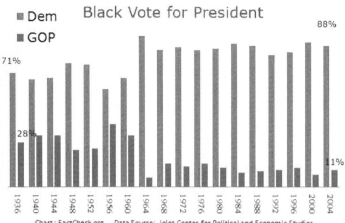

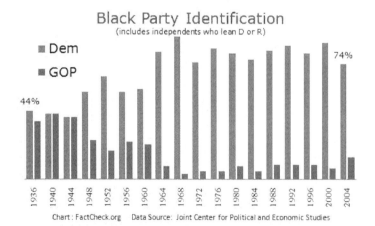

Popular black votes by parties in US elections
from the 1930s through 2004.

The narrative that blacks support the Democrats because of the mistreatment of blacks by racist Republicans has dominated black culture; however, as noted above, to make such a statement is a mischaracterization of the facts. I believe that Democrats have been able to hide behind handouts, starting with the New Deal.

The Democrats realized that as long as they could give away free stuff to blacks, they would keep getting black votes, and they could hide their shameful history of bigotry, staying in the shadows. Further, when white and black Democrats want black votes, the race card is played, and it works with significant effect.

Now contrast the scenario I am about to describe with that of President Lyndon B. Johnson, a Democrat whose comments about black people was especially derogatory. Johnson referred to bills favoring blacks as "nigger bills." Our current president, Donald J. Trump, allegedly made derogatory comments during a closed-door meeting on Deferred Action for Childhood Arrivals (DACA) about people in America with temporary protected status (TPS), saying some immigrants are from "shitholes countries," a statement he denies making. However, the reaction has been vicious. Should the president speak like that? If he did, he should not! This is not a defense of the president as he is well able to defend himself.

This is race baiting by the Democrats. In my opinion, the point of making this alleged comment public was to prove that the president is a racist. That goes with the underhanded tactics used when Democrats are trying to force a political narrative along racial lines: "just say racism" and conservatives will back off because they do not want to be called racist.

Illinois Senator Dick Durbin, who allegedly made those statements to the media about Trump's DACA comments, has been known to lie about details of private meetings. I believe he was politicizing the event. He intended to hurt people in such a way that they would react with anger and outrage. This is simply another example of how Democrats will go to any length and to any cost to get votes, regardless of how it affects anyone. Such a man should not be invited to a private meeting with anyone.

I further believe that kind of deception is toxic and shows the Democratic Party's willingness to use deception and emotions to sway public opinion. When the Democrats had power in Congress in 2015 to pass a law helping DACA recipients, they did not. However, with the 2018 midterm elections on the horizon, they are now acting as if they care about the DACA issue.

Immigrants have made many significant contributions to this country. Those from the West Indies and African nations in particular have often pursued higher education and become productive, first-class citizens of this country, not depending on welfare.

Word of caution to immigrants: I understand having legal status in a country you love is important. However, please pay attention to the Democratic Party's history with black Americans, a history of promising much but delivering little of substance. It is imperative not to buy into the notion that Democrats can fix your every problem.

Most immigrants who have made it to the shores of America are hardworking people who only want opportunities, not handouts. Handouts are a trap of truly living the American dream: it may feel good at first, but in the end it takes full control of your life, leaving you dependent on the government like an addict. As an immigrant, I want to see the situation resolved in the best way possible. I believe these issues should be dealt with in a way that all can be comfortable, however uncomfortable the meetings are. When a lawmaker comes out and makes a statement as Durbin did, it does nothing to help the process.

I believe immigrants wanting to come to America should be given a chance to come as long as they do not become a burden to the state and pose a danger to national security. Having a merit-based immigration system based on abilities, not on country of origin, would be beneficial to America. Immigrants should be willing to assimilate into American culture and ideologies, and I believe most immigrants who come here want to make America a better country. After all, some are from terrible places.

By merely being white in America, it is automatically assumed that you are racist. You are then blamed for racism or accused of having an unfair advantage in making economic progress. That makes the Democrats' shenanigans harder to detect, but I am hoping that will no longer be the case.

The Democrats were just in the right place at the right time. They had a presidential candidate in the '60s who signed off on the Civil Rights bill that was supported by a majority of Republicans in Congress, but it is the Democratic Party that has the true prejudicial platform. Most whites, especially Republicans, are looked at with an air of suspicion and, sadly, most blacks in their state of anger believe the lie, making it harder for true American conciliation.

I will end this chapter with a quote from Frederick Douglas: "I knew that however bad the Republican Party was, the Democratic Party was much worse. The elements of which the Republican party was composed gave better ground for the ultimate hope of the success of the colored man's cause than those of the Democratic party." That was true then, and it is true now.

CHAPTER 2

The Black Family and the Church

● ● ●

WHEN THE EUROPEANS FIRST DECIDED to explore the New World, it was to spread the gospel for the Catholic Church. After coming in contact with the Indians, missionaries made it their purpose to spread the gospel to them. However, the Europeans wanted to develop the plantations, and the Indians were not equipped to handle the harsh labor conditions.

It was suggested that Africans would be better suited for the plantations. The Africans were never thought of as interested in the Christian religion, and the Europeans knew that exposing African slaves to Christianity would help them see that slavery was wrong. So when the Africans were brought to the Americas it was thought best to indoctrinate them in nominal Christianity. That satisfied some of the settlers who felt it was not right to educate Africans as they were considered to be more like animals than fellow human beings.

Still, there always was an interest in proselytizing to the slaves about Christianity in early America. However, plantation owners knew that true understanding of the gospel by the slaves could mobilize slaves to advocate for their freedom.

There was a small minority of white Christians who wanted the end of slavery. They believed that all men are born free. Some early white missionaries believed the only way to convert the slaves was to set them free. Those missionaries went about preaching against all forms of evil, especially the institution of slavery.

In the 1770s missionaries aggressively attacked the institution of slavery, forcing the church to make a stand; some churches even required that itinerant preachers set their slaves free because slavery was against God's laws. Those missionaries believed that slavery was wrong and should be banished from the American colonies.

There are some in today's society who preach that Christianity is the white man's religion that was used to indoctrinate the slaves to keep them in bondage. However, while there is some truth to those statements, that narrative is mostly false because many Christians vehemently opposed slavery. Christianity is an Eastern religion. Through the church, it was established that all men are created equal by God with unalienable rights that should not be infringed upon by anyone.

Even during slavery, freed blacks and slaves were able to minister to both slaves and free blacks along with whites because of their understanding of the gospel and preaching power. Some slaves became so influential in their preaching that they were able to secure their freedom and that of their families. Some also received acceptance and respect among the white community. However, the ability to preach became restricted in some quarters, especially after Nat Turner's rebellion.

The Church

Blacks, especially those in the North, found that some of the churches they attended were not particularly welcoming or friendly toward them. In the South, blacks were limited in their choices of worship. Also, in most mixed-congregation churches, blacks were relegated to the back pews.

The first independent black church started in Savannah, Georgia, unofficially, in the late eighteenth century under the leadership of George Liele, who was succeeded by Andrew Bryan after Liele left for Jamaica. It was not until 1786 that an official black church was established through Richard Allen in Philadelphia. Allen saw that blacks had special needs and wanted to address those needs as blacks did not have a place of worship. Allen started a Bible study and soon had forty-two members; that encouraged him to ask for a separate place of worship for blacks. He was not helped. It was only through his preaching power that he was able to change people's minds to support him. Allen eventually succeeded in organizing Bethel AME Church in 1794. Many other black churches followed.

During the Civil War the Christian religion was put to the guns and cannons, and it divided the church. Many fought to end the institution of slavery as they believed that God intended man not only to be free in mind but also in body. Many hoped that the Civil War was the final blow to the wretched institution of slavery and watched in awe as the hand of God delivered them from that wicked oppression.

Many blacks left the pulpit and the protection of the church to fight with the Union Army. To some, the war was not a religious one, but to many blacks, justice had finally come to the Southern States that fought to uphold slavery.

After emancipation in 1865, the church was where blacks could freely socialize and learn to read. Through the church, many freed blacks learned to think freely and educate themselves. The Bible, the most available book to the free blacks, made a great impression on how black families viewed the world and helped them develop literature and philosophy.

It was not foreign for blacks to be able to recite whole books of the Bible. Furthermore, blacks developed excellent oratorical skills and ethics from studying the Bible. The church taught blacks that they could be independent and that they did not have to rely on white support during periods of hardship or turbulent times. As is the case today, those who are more dependent on the government for economic and social support are more vulnerable. They are at more of a disadvantage in making any societal progress. The church in the years after emancipation realized that if it could develop men and women of good character and influence, then it could influence their communities for good, both politically and educationally. The position of many in the church was not to let men destroy themselves, and they believed that a strong emphasis on the gospel could help accomplish that goal.

Today we can see that many black Christians have aligned themselves with a political party that wants to keep them poor, ignorant, and broke, both spiritually and financially.

The church has produced some people with integrity who aroused and fought for the causes of the newly-free blacks. Some of those men were elected to political offices; others made educating the race their number one priority. Out of the church arose Martin Luther King Jr. who fought valiantly to end segregation in the middle of the twentieth century.

The church has always been a beacon of light in America and in the black community. During Reconstruction, the church symbolized pride, freedom, and a sense of control. The church is where black America first found its voice in this country. However, most of those voices have been silenced in the black community today through political correctness or not wanting to upset popular culture.

There is another factor at play also: the purpose that the church leaders once served in the early years before and after the Civil War and Jim Crow was to be a voice for the helpless. That voice has now been hijacked by race hustlers who seek to keep blacks angry, ignorant, and disenfranchised. They continue collecting money from white liberals, telling blacks they are the only ones who can go to the white man's table and speak to him.

Those hucksters are the new order of the day and will do anything for money. They do not seek to educate the black man to maintain his family or become knowledgeable about economics and politics.

The most significant destruction of the black community in America is happening in the black family; fix the family, and you will fix most of the impoverished and menial positions that now plague the black community. I repeat: the church is where blacks found their voice and were reassured of their God-given, intrinsic worth. The church laid that foundation for the freedom we all now enjoy.

THE BLACK FAMILY

Slavery, systemic racism, and Jim Crow are blamed for the chaos in many black families today. I believe that is untrue; again, the statistics and facts do not support such a narrative. Even with the severe hardship of slavery when slave marriages had no legal protection or recognition, families stayed intact.

Slaves lived under the constant threat of family breakup by the sale of loved ones, and loved ones were often sold to defray plantation debt. When deemed a danger to plantation life, selling slaves was also used as a means to keep slaves submissive. However, slaves did their best to keep marriages and families together, even though slave marriages may not have been recognized by slave owners or others in the country. Slavery violated the first created purpose of marriage—honoring the family.

Marriage is not a construct of government or a group of people but a union granted by God. Marriage was the first institution God created in the Garden of Eden. All other systems follow marriage, and society's values should reflect those values that support the family first.

As the Civil War dismantled the system of slavery, freed slaves went about searching for loved ones, often through much difficulty, to reunite their families. In contrast, today's society and government have made it difficult for families to stay together. Usually, once there is separation it becomes a permanent rift that leads to many injuries to those affected. Also, after the Civil War black families went about formally legalizing their marriages. Early black families in America had a strong commitment to family and the church.

One of the most significant leftist attacks on the church has been the idea of gay marriage, and it seems to have significant support from some in the black community—even ministers. Scientifically and biblically, there are no significant benefits to the government from same-sex marriages. When governments decide what constitutes a marriage through laws, it is bad for nations. More laws morph into something else, eventually leading to an unrecognizable institution.

As I have stated earlier, marriage is the institution that forms governments. Marriage between a man and a woman is the institution that continues new generations; if fewer children are being born, then society will have fewer people to put into the economy of a state, just like abortion is bad for society as it reduces the population of future generations.

Take Social Security. If a society does not have enough productive members to replace the old and dying, then that society will eventually collapse. Another one of the left's arguments equates gay marriage opposition with being black or with the discrimination blacks faced during Jim Crow and the ban on interracial marriages. That is deeply offensive, to say the least, as your color is sacred and immutable. Secondly, those prohibitions were a direct attack on human liberty.

Black leadership should be advocating for stronger family relationships rather than pushing the idea of marriage equality. Our government already has enough laws to protect the most vulnerable. All people have a right to live the way they want to live, and no one should be forced to accept rules contrary to their nature or beliefs. Protection of our trust in the institution of marriage should not be seen as an attack on anyone's sexual freedom. My faith in marriage denies no one the equal protection under the law that is guaranteed in this country.

Democrats are pushing to redefine the institution of marriage and have gained tremendous support from some in the black community, even some in the church. This is not the Democratic Party's first rodeo when it comes to marriage; it was also the party that did not want to honor interracial marriages before and after the Civil War for the newly freed slaves. That opposition was eventually overturned.

A further demise of marriage is the government incentives that have replaced men in homes. Some men, being weak, gladly surrender their rights of parenting to the government. We know that sometimes the government removes the rights of a parent due to abuse of children, but that is not the focus of this book. The ruling by the Supreme Court on marriage equality has put the most potent advocate for the black community in the leftist firing line. Now laws can be passed to restrict the messages that are preached from the pulpit with severe consequences.

The black community must be reminded that even with the history or the abuse of some in the church to justify slavery and other atrocities, the church was the most prominent and most potent force against the evil institution of slavery and Jim Crow. So partnering with a political party that can take away your rights as to how you worship and live your life is bad for America.

According to statistics from the 1938 Encyclopedia of Social Sciences, only 11 percent of children born into black families were born out of wedlock; that was five years after President Franklin Roosevelt's New Deal. By 1960 that number had doubled to 22 percent. By 2017, the number was 77 percent, according to a Washington *Examiner* article dated May 5, 2017. In contrast, according to the National Center for Health Statistics, whites born out of wedlock more than doubled from 3.2 percent in 1938 to 9.6 percent in 1960, and the percentage is 29.4 today.

The argument is that systemic racism, slavery, and Jim Crow are responsible for the increase in out-of-marriage births. But that cannot be true because, during those periods, the black family was much stronger and was facing untold oppression by the legal system, yet the family stayed together. So what would you say is contributing to this destruction of black people in America? I will say it is weak family structure and government dependence.

Marriage breakdown hurts the least fortunate the most; in fact, intact marriages reduce child poverty by as much as 80 percent. The fact that the white families out of wedlock rates more than doubled during that period is pointing to something else. The common denominator is the massive social programs through the New Deal. A Brookings Institution study conducted between 1970 and 1996 found that $226 billion was spent on social welfare programs as a result of the breakdown of marriages. The result of that failure is high teen pregnancy, high crime rates, and increased poverty. *Let's be clear: I am not saying lives were better for blacks during slavery and Jim Crow; it just shows that, even with severe oppression, the family stayed intact.*

Finally, there is often talk of separation of church and state when the Christian religion is brought up in a conversation dealing with matters in the public square. Liberals want all references to God removed from the public and government spaces. It is said that we should leave our religion at home. This example might be simplistic, but if my belief tells me stealing is wrong, should I forget that when I am in public?

And how can there be a separation of church and state? When politicians (potential state representatives) have made the church their stomping grounds, and there is hardly ever an election result that has not been determined by those in the church.

The First Amendment states, "Congress shall make no law respecting an establishment of religion, or prohibiting the free exercise thereof," which I understand to mean that government cannot establish a national religion, but neither can it prevent citizens from displaying their religious beliefs in public spaces.

Blacks, I believe, have paid the dearest price by wrongly supporting a political party that cares nothing about their most precious symbol of hope—God and the church. Or have most blacks forgotten who God is? For the black churches that have aligned themselves with senseless liberal agendas to regain credibility, they will have to move away from such groups and stop taking contributions from them. To the black community, the church is light, and light cannot exist or partner with darkness.

CHAPTER 3

Black Education

● ● ●

THE PURPOSE OF EDUCATION IS to teach you to think, question, and even doubt. If you are unable to think for yourself in a logical, consistent manner, you are at the mercy of those who control mass media.

Some in control of mass media believe they should always be pushing the narratives of the arts (music and TV), beliefs, and politics in every facet of our lives. If you do not pull yourself away from such media, you become a zombie or an intellectual slave, regurgitating material without thinking of the consequences, the sources, or the purpose of such information.

How did we allow this to happen? Education, not indoctrination, was always valuable to blacks during and after slavery, so why have so many blacks allowed themselves to become intellectual slaves to white liberals and socialistic agendas? The drive to educate the black man was led by the independent black church after slavery ended.

Churches were not merely places of worship; they also served as the schools and the civic centers. During Reconstruction the church affected many lives by teaching blacks how to educate themselves. That was not a government-run institution but well-intentioned people wanting to improve the conditions of the newly-freed slaves. Today, in some ways, some churches still do their best to push education, but they do so with considerable opposition from government-instituted mandates, primarily by some in the public education sectors.

Teaching has now become a social phenomenon whereby it is more about not offending others than a process of learning. Some courses push mainly leftist agendas of erasing past symbols and rewriting the history of perceived wrongs. For instance, pulling down Confederate statues does nothing to help the current poor conditions of some blacks; in fact, it costs money to do so.

History is there for us to learn from, and wrong information does need to be corrected. Rewriting the past to suit our likings will not affect the history, yet the danger is that people will use the past as an excuse to carry out evil social agendas under the guise of correcting those wrongs.

Public education has its roots in socialism. I was a beneficiary of public education early in my life; however, I found my footing in a privately run educational system.

Public institutions not kept in check eventually become extensions of government agendas and are ultimately used as indoctrination tools, as we are now witnessing in many of America's public schools.

Kids are now taught confusing sex education and are encouraged not to offend someone because that person is confused about who he or she is. Is gender identity biologically determined and cannot change? Does how one feels about oneself define reality? If people are free to choose how they identify, why impose the idea of their existence on others? Those questions need to be answered. How can it be argued that science makes gender identity unchangeable but not biological sex (male/female)? Does feeling like a man make a woman a man? Likewise, does feeling like a woman make a man a woman? Sadly, I believe that if these trends continue it will lead to the weakening of this great republic.

A further demise of education is that unions protect less-than-satisfactory teachers. Further, open display of religion is discouraged. Christian students are under constant assault. In many left-leaning—and even in some right-leaning institutions—any ideas that do not align with popular thoughts are ridiculed.

Also, though opinions are not equal, they all deserve to be heard, and students should be allowed to make decisions based on facts, not feelings. Teachers and professors who continue to push leftist agendas should not be allowed to use threats of failing students to force those students to accept their ridiculous viewpoints. Students should be protected from such abuses.

As you will see below, I believe it is always the responsibility of the parents, not the government, to educate their children to be productive members of society. Leaving the education of your children solely to the government is borderline child abuse. It is not the government's responsibility to teach your children about morality or how to read and write.

A few years ago I attended an NAACP meeting in a city near where I live. I listened to many who were present. The constant theme was needing more money and better teachers to help failing students perform better. However, the glaring factor was that the school district was not poor and had a large budget. I noticed that most of the parents present at that NAACP meeting had children who were performing well; however, a majority of the problem students' parents were missing.

I inquired about the parents who were absent and was challenged by a former politician who seemed stuck on the idea that money and racial inequality were the reasons for such failures. No one present seemed to say much about the missing parents and that the major breakdown of poor education is due to broken homes and the lack of parental motivation to instill strong learning habits in their children.

Even the least educated in a two-parent home with a strong work ethic and a commitment to their children's education can produce some of the most brilliant minds and productive members of society. This is not an attack on single parenting but an assertion that the premise of society is formed on the idea of two parents—a man and a woman—and that children are more mentally and emotionally stable in such households.

Schools in majority-black areas are consistently at the bottom of the educational spectrum. The failure of such institutions is often blamed on racism. However, even with large sums of money from governments, these schools continue to fail. I believe that parents should advocate for more voucher programs that would allow them to pull their children out of failing schools and send them to more productive institutions. Failing schools should not continue to abuse children into ignorance. For the voucher program to work efficiently there has to be a balance of a paying population versus voucher recipients. Otherwise, those schools' performances will be no better than that of public schools.

Parents should also consider homeschooling their children when possible as their children are likely to outperform most students and their peers in public schools, even when their parents possess only a moderate education.

The other option is introducing merit-based programs within school districts, allowing less government control over where children are placed in schools. Those should be based on performance and abilities only.

Make trade school an option. For instance, if children want to learn a trade, then their emphasis should be geared toward that at the high school level, which would eventually send more skilled eighteen- and nineteen-year-old workers into the workforce with higher earning potentials.

As parents, we should understand that not everyone matures at the same rate, and forcing children to take courses they are not interested in so they can work at the corner store earning minimum wage with bad attitudes is not encouraging.

I believe such a system would greatly benefit the black community as black youths would not feel that colleges selling worthless degrees, fast-food restaurants, and the corner stores are their only options for earning a living.

The beauty of being in America, more than anywhere else in the world, is that students can study a trade in high school and pursue that for a while. If students later decide to go to college or pursue a different career path, they can do so without incurring significant loan debt because they would have had a career and, hopefully, people would be more mature and able to handle the pressures of earning a degree in a college setting.

Lastly, we educate our children to think for themselves and make rational decisions. However, so many voices in the black communities have been silenced by community spokespersons who claim to have the know-how to sit down with the white man. Such persons continue to spew that narrative as community activists and, for the most part, they and their cronies are the only ones benefiting. It is time that blacks break out of that mindset and realize that, with confidence and sincerity, they can approach anyone or any situation without seeking a loudmouth and, for the most part, they will get better results than anyone else could.

In summary, proper education should be the focus of making children productive adults. Parents should not be afraid to pull children from failing schools. Giving more money to schools does not solve a lack of parental commitment to their children's educations. And lastly, knowledge should help you think as an individual, not as an intellectual slave.

CHAPTER 4

History of Black Conservatives and Successes

● ● ●

He was born a slave in Franklin County, Virginia, in the most miserable, desolate, and discouraging conditions, according to the words of Booker T. Washington. He knew nothing of his ancestry and not much of his father. There were no memories of a family sitting around a table enjoying a meal and each other. But even with the harshness of slavery, Washington harbored no bitterness toward whites. After the Civil War ended slavery, Booker T. had an intense yearning to learn to read and would read anything he could get in his hands. Sometime during his boyhood, his mother was able to secure a book for him, and he devoured it—and that was without a teacher.

One thing that was as true then as it is today was that Washington noticed that when he was in school, other students focused solely on material things and made fun of him for not being able to afford fancy new things. He said of them, "They have ended up in the penitentiary, while others are not able to buy any of those finer things." Washington tried to picture himself coming from a long line of distinguished ancestry going back hundreds of years with a proud name and being a member of the popular race, but eventually he concluded that with such leanings he would have depended on ancestry and color to do what he should do for himself.

In other words, he accepted where he was but used that position to better himself instead of being the beneficiary of an inheritance. That was such a profound statement by a man born a slave who realized that, with his freedom, he could accomplish great things, and that is what he set out to do. He believed in having a sense of ancestry but not in overly relying on it. He thought whites had a sense of community and, in striving for success, he did not want to disappoint that community or disgrace it. Blacks, for the most part, did not have that shared sense of community in his time to keep the community striving for good. Booker T. Washington believed that success is not the place one occupies in life but the obstacles one has to overcome while trying to succeed.

On his way to the Hampton Institute to educate himself he survived on only prayer and hope; penniless, dirty, hungry, and sleeping on the sides of streets Washington found there were many obstacles to overcome. He saw the harsh struggles and knew that black youths had to work harder for recognition than whites did. However, that created an advantage for him as those struggles helped develop strength and character. He learned to be meticulous in performing his tasks, and when he eventually reached Hampton Institute and was seeking admission, he had the opportunity to clean a classroom, which impressed a member of the staff, who gave him a chance to start his studies there.

Washington completed his studies and ended in Tuskegee, Alabama, the Black Belt of the South, so named because of the soil found in the area. Washington was the primary driver of the prestigious Tuskegee Institute, which started in a stable and a hen house in 1881. He focused on teaching practical skills useful to the everyday man, so students farmed their food and built their buildings. He traveled far and wide to raise funding for new buildings and for tuition. He was a firm believer that education was the best route for the advancement of blacks. At the time of his death in 1915, he left Tuskegee on solid footing and was honored in 1940 as the first black to appear on a US postage stamp.

Also born into slavery in Missouri near the end of the Civil War, as his biography states, George Washington Carver decided to head for Kansas at age twelve, seeking better fortune and wanting to educate himself. For fourteen years he drifted throughout the Kansas plains, learning about the vast grasslands, different plants, the soil, and the people.

He tried his hand at many things; he was good at ironing and cooking and was able to survive using those skills, but just like Washington, he had a burning desire to learn and a passion for God. After being rejected due to his color from the first school he applied to, Highland College in Highland, Kansas, he got his start at Simpson College in Indianola, Iowa. Carver thrived at Simpson College, and his stellar character won him many admirers. He loved plants and painting and was encouraged to use his love of plants to study botany.

After Simpson, Carver was accepted at Iowa State University to study botany, and he became one of the nation's premier horticulturists. His excellent reputation in Iowa grew to the point that any new student who believed he could antagonize him because of his color drew rude reprisals from other students.

Carver won many awards in Iowa and was noticed by Washington. The head of the Tuskegee Institute wanted Carver to serve as a member of his staff while leading the agricultural department. His strong relationship with James Wilson, US Secretary of Agriculture between 1897 and 1913, while he was at Iowa helped him significantly while he was at Tuskegee. It also helped Washington secure support and a visit to Tuskegee by President William McKinley, giving great visibility to the institute.

Carver was able to develop many uses for peanuts, and his effect on the US Congress did not go unnoticed. He was instrumental in establishing the agricultural economy in the South. He advised the likes of Henry Ford and Presidents Teddy Roosevelt, Franklin Roosevelt, and Calvin Coolidge. After his death in 1943, the George Washington Carver Monument was constructed in Missouri in his honor, the first for any black or nonpresident.

"Finally, we are challenged to dedicate our lives to the cause of Christ even as communists dedicate theirs to communism," said Martin Luther King Jr. "We who cannot accept the creed of the communists recognize their zeal and commitment to a cause that they believe will create a better world. They have a sense and purpose and destiny, and they work passionately and assiduously to win others to communism . . . We have neither zeal for Christ nor zest for his kingdom . . . the church is little more than a secular social club having a thin veneer of religiosity."

Karl Marx, the founder of Marxism, stated his philosophies were incompatible with Christian beliefs. Martin Luther King Jr. was also a believer that communism and Christianity are incompatible; he was later branded a communist sympathizer. However, that was an incorrect assessment of a man who knew the dangers that communism posed to the church and to America. The very instrument he was able to use to advocate for equality for blacks, the church, could not be as powerful under communism. Under communism, the state is a god. He also recognized that black Americans were in danger of being used to further communist agendas under the guise of equality. So much of today's so-called civil rights movements, such as Black Lives Matter, are based on those principles.

Black Lives Matter is supposed to agitate for justice against perceived police brutality against black men. However, if members of that group were really about the protection of life, they would be in the streets marching for the most innocent, the many unborn babies aborted in the black community. You cannot honestly care about life outside the womb when you have no concern for how life is formed or don't care to protect it at its most innocent and helpless stage.

I believe that Black Lives Matter is here only to push leftist, hate-filled agendas against police while building up its coffers. Not many black leaders today have presented the real dangers of the ideology of communism or socialism to the black community, and because most black leaders are Democrats, it may never happen. That would go against most of their core beliefs, and if they were to do so, they would become outcasts.

A system based on materialism and humanism has weaved its way into black America, something that Martin Luther King Jr., one of America's most recognized black conservatives, had warned about. His successes need not be elaborated; the proof is that he gave his life in his tireless and relentless march for black equality under the laws of God and the US Constitution.

Highways, schools, holidays, and monuments have been named after him and built in his honor. His legendary "I Have a Dream" speech is one of the most-quoted speeches of all time and is often used when someone is trying to woo black voters. However, one of the most glaring omissions of who Martin Luther King Jr. was is the belief that shaped his worldviews, irrespective of one's opinion of him. It was not Marxism or his color but his quest for justice, his faith in God the Creator, and his quest to expose evil. His worldview was entirely Christian, and through those lenses he anchored his mission to march for justice for marginalized black Americans.

Justice is color blind and, as such, we should strive to root out evil among ourselves so we do not become part of the ploy of those seeking to control us. King is a stalwart and true American success story for many to emulate. He succeeded at a time when the laws of the land were against the black race. There was no affirmative action to get him in. King had to fight to succeed, and he did succeed.

When the bar is lowered to facilitate those who are lagging, not because of physical or mental abilities, those competing at the lower bars will always be left wanting, feeling cheated, and never completed because they have been abused and duped into thinking that the way to success is setting the bar lower.

Sadly, there will be a gap that will never close because those at the lower bars start believing that clearing those will place them on the same podium as those who have achieved greater heights. That is the disparity between whites and blacks in America, a gap that can be closed only by each man's willingness to sacrifice for the good of his family.

Man is not the master of the universe, and if blacks are to succeed in building solid foundations for success, then going back to the root of success is imperative: God, man (husband), woman (wife), children, and then government. It is "we the people" who come first, not "we the government." It is on the principle of the family that government was formed to protect our dearest needs. Men aspire to do great things and to build, protect, and secure. On these principles lies success that no government should impede, and the men described above achieved great success despite government impediments.

CHAPTER 5

Victimization and Postmodernism in Black America

● ● ●

IT IS OFTEN SAID THAT slavery, Jim Crow, and racism are the reasons that blacks are living in deplorable conditions, hold dead-end jobs, and can't get ahead. The laws of the states encourage systemic racism; black men are incarcerated more than any other group. Lastly, blacks suffer more than anyone else from police brutality. Sound familiar? If it does, it is because those words are often used to turn out black support for Democratic candidates when candidates have nothing to offer constituents. They can always count on those proven tactics to do the trick.

"If you repeat a lie often enough, people will believe it, and you will even come to believe it yourself," infamous Nazi propagandist Joseph Goebbels said. The Nazi propaganda machine also said, "Propaganda works best when those who are being manipulated are confident they are acting on their own free will. This is the secret of propaganda: Those who are to be persuaded by it should be completely immersed in the ideas of the propaganda without ever noticing that they are being immersed in it. Propaganda must facilitate the displacement of aggression by specifying the targets for hatred."

Before I address those issues further, I will start with what is a law and what are rights and how laws are supposed to work in government. These are my interpretations and understandings.

Law is a force given to a group by society to enforce justice. Rights are our created purpose given to us by God. The goal of laws is to protect natural rights. Our natural rights are life, liberty, and property. By law, we can use force to defend ourselves, our property, and our freedom. When laws deviate from those purposes, they become corrupted. Slavery and Jim Crow violate freedom, taxes violate property, and murder violates life. Communities can come together and form groups such as a police force to protect our natural rights.

We deviate from protecting natural rights when we create laws that encroach on liberty and property. Forcing people to accept a perceived view with the consequence of depriving them of property—pushing bakers to make cakes for an event they do not want to take part in and fining them for not doing it—is one example.

The scenario described above shows that laws have become corrupt and have moved away from their primary purposes. Furthermore, those rules are now protected by the states, giving them legal standing. Those regulations further encourage others to follow suit, making more unjust rulings because this was not dismissed. The moment such a potential law (laws forcing people to provide services that are against their sincerely held beliefs) rears its ugly head, it gives rise to corruption.

Any act, whether under the guise of providing social help or education, can become perverted. Laws used to take from someone or some entity to provide social services or enrich others are a significant page out of the socialism playbook and should be discouraged at all times.

Blacks have been told that for them to improve their conditions, they need to have legislative representatives advocating for their causes. Those legislators then help create laws that give them more freedom, but laws do not give us more freedom, they restrict it. When representatives advocate for more laws to help level the playing fields for blacks, that kind of thinking should be discouraged. As stated above, the purpose of laws is to protect our natural rights; when our natural rights are protected, we are free to live how we want and do as we like without fear of the state. Under such a system all people are responsible for themselves and their families; success is driven by their ability to provide and care for themselves.

Forcing someone to take on someone else's responsibility is unjust and should not be encouraged. How can I say that? Supporting people who are not fully able to take care of themselves is a noble cause. Even though it seems like the right thing to do, caring for such people has to come from the natural goodness of one's heart, not from the government. Humans are naturally selfish and should not be forced to do things against their will. When governments take control of redistributing wealth, it gets abused. Wealth then is at the mercy of those who are in power, so the abuse of those in need continues.

The laws abolishing slavery were ratified by the Thirteenth and Fourteenth Amendments in 1865 and 1868, respectively. That was followed by the Civil Rights Act of 1964. Those laws protect our liberties. The Second Amendment gives us the right to defend our person. The Fourth Amendment provides us with the right to defend our property. So what do we need legislators for? We already have full protection as provided by our Constitution. Are our legislators there to uphold laws or to pervert justice?

The responsibilities of our legislators then become minimal and, in most cases, unnecessary, thus reducing the size of government. We do not need charlatans or spokespersons advocating for rights we already possess; what we need are more people standing up for what is right while providing for the family. We have to understand that with the protection of our persons by the law as guaranteed by the Constitution we will have to move beyond the process of victimization. The law is doing what it is supposed to do: it is giving us protection to carry out our human functions. The law cannot redress inequalities by forcing others to pay for level playing fields or to feel guilty about racism and past wrongs of others; if it does, it becomes a perversion and an arm for those in power—or those seeking power—to abuse those they disagree with.

So how do the laws deal with the high incarceration rates for blacks? Justice is color blind, and if you violate a person or property, then the law is there to prevent that. Without the perversion of the process, what other reasons are there for the high incarceration rates of black men? Could it be a breakdown in the family structure or a lack of morality, or could it be the lack of respect for other people's liberties?

When we agitate for justice, we first must honestly address the causes and be honest with the process. Could fewer black men be incarcerated? The answer is yes. Now the other question is, could fewer black men be jailed without violating the natural rights of people's due process? That is a question to ponder. If the law operates in its purest form by allowing for due process, soon we will have to address the real issues for the high number of incarcerations. Again, I believe the main issue is weak family structure.

POSTMODERNISM

Postmodernism is not a new phenomenon by any stretch, but lately it is coming to full light. There is a hunger to connect to the past in black America (roots in Africa), so much so that rationalism is being substituted for humanistic beliefs and naturalism/secularism. You will hear, as I noted earlier, some in professional black circles say that Christianity or Judeo-Christian belief is the white man's religion because some used it as a means to justify slavery. We should move away from such beliefs and embrace a more skeptical and humanistic way of thinking. Some of the beliefs now embraced include the following:

- Naturalism teaches that science provides answers to all there is to life.
- Secularism teaches that we are merely matter floating about in space and time.
- Atheism teaches the cold revulsion and denial of God or the concept of God.

According to the naturalists, we simply happen to be here, and life is only a series of random events. So in essence, we are not responsible for our actions because those events are predetermined. If those philosophies are to be believed, then why the outrage? After all, we are only matter floating around in space and time. I must further point out that these latter systems of belief and other religions were around during slavery and played no significant role in bringing down that evil institution.

Imagine a slave owner believing that he was within his rights to maintain slavery; how could we use moral relativism or atheism to argue that such evil should end? Seeing that relativism asserts that you live by your own set of rules, how could you say that the slave owner was wrong? And with atheism, how do you convince someone that slavery is evil when the atheist believes there is no objective moral Law Giver and that morality evolves? When would atheism develop to the point of acknowledging the evils of slavery—when public opinion about what is evil changes? As of today, atheism cannot offer a strong argument for the origin of morality; however, the church can.

That is postmodernism in a nutshell—breaking from past beliefs in the absolute and objective moral order for a more relativistic way of living or the feeling that you are the reality you create and that you live by your truths. How we combat that is a tough task, but the way I see it and have implied throughout this book is that, without the Christian religion, the American Constitution would not have been as strong. Slavery and Jim Crow, I believe, would have been harder to eradicate in America as no other belief system provides for what Christianity has done in the West—including ending slavery.

One only has to look in places where many of the beliefs or ideologies other than Christianity are actively practiced to see the treatment of inequality. In America, understanding the Constitution and the law of the land in this great democratic republic will give you a much better platform for genuinely living in freedom, and it also will provide better opportunities to provide for yourself and your family.

CHAPTER 6

Moving beyond the Pain

● ● ●

It is often said we do not understand the pain of the slaves, the suffering under the evil system of Jim Crow, or how systemic racism has relegated blacks to second-class citizenship or kept them from promotions at work. Those are often the lines used by people who seem trapped in the hurt of past wrongs. Most of us did not experience or live in those times. I must say I am thankful I did not.

As I said earlier, when we attempt to put ourselves in the past we tend to use our current understanding of life to make judgments on the history based on our present conditions. We have to be careful when we go down that road as the past exists no more, and the only guide to it is what history or our sometimes-good sometimes-flawed experiences tell us. What we must do is learn from the past so as not to make those same mistakes.

Our pain, anger, and resentment tend to come from those closest to us. Our reactions to most situations are a projection of those past hurts and bitterness. If we are honest with ourselves, it is best to forgive and move on. Forgiving allows us to better deal with outside pressures. However, if those feelings of hopelessness are not addressed, then when we get involved in challenging situations, we are more likely to react emotionally and irrationally, skewing our perception of the reality of the situation.

We were created to be rational beings, not emotional creatures, for in rationality there is the force of love and proper emotions to function within the human family.

Being a black conservative in America, you should not carry a stigma or live in fear of castration. The black conservatives, I believe, hold the key to the black revolution and the uplifting of the black family.

We are not sellouts, Uncle Toms, or blacks acting as whites; we are Americans who believe in freedom, individualism, and doing the right thing. We all have to come to the understanding that the state cannot fix our most profound problems. To grow, we have to divorce ourselves from those politicians and those in the media who continue to spew wrong information, thinking they are sincere while only creating more anxiety.

People form nations, states, or governments; if the people are poor, then the state will be weak. A country can remain prosperous only if most of its citizens are productive members. The best way for this to happen is to allow capitalism to work with less restrictive policies. If families are broken, then the state will be broken, as I said above. "We the people" form governments. So to believe the lies that the state is the way to level the playing field for equality and make us more prosperous is not wise.

The state is an organization representing members of society for the common good—the protection of life, liberty, and property. If you want to be prosperous, you have to go it alone; no one else knows or sees your dreams, so do not be fooled into believing that anyone else has your best interests at heart. Anyone, including any political party, who engages in identity politics (black or white) should be avoided. Identity politics is bad for any society.

Stand up for what is right. Breakaway from noxious thinking, and you will, indeed, live the American dream—not as an outcast but as a full-blooded American exemplifying e pluribus unum.

QUESTIONS

● ● ●

I HAVE BEEN ASKED THIS question many times, and I am sure it will come up. How do you call yourself a Christian and support policies of a president who has been married thrice, among other things? I will first point out the story of Oskar Schindler. He was considered a womanizer while many Nazis were men who honored family values but also committed grave atrocities against the Jews. Schindler, however, risked everything to save many Jews. Who determines self-worth or what is right? Were the Nazis good people?

According to the Bible, Rahab, the harlot, opened her home to Jewish spies and risked her life to save them when they were spying out the Promised Land. Should the Jews have refused her help?

Another question that comes up in political conversation is who I voted for. If you were drowning and I could save you, would it matter who I voted for?

Lastly, my book is not about how the president won the presidency; it is about why my views have changed, and why I left the Democratic Party.

●　●　●

CLASTON A. BERNARD WAS BORN in Jamaica and later immigrated to the United States. He is now an American citizen and careful observer of American politics.

Bernard received his degree in human resource management from Louisiana State University. He is a 2002 Commonwealth Games decathlon champion, national collegiate champion, four-time Southeastern Conference champion, and two-time Olympian.

SOURCES

Bastiat, Frederic. *The Law.* Baltimore: Laissez Faire Books, 2015.

Bositis, David A. "Blacks and the 2004 Democratic National Convention." *Joint Center for Political and Economic Studies(2004)*: 9.

———. "The Black Vote in 2004," *Joint Center for Political and Economic Studies* (2005):

Carver, George Washington. *Natural-born Genius.* Lexington: Wild Centuries Press, 1998.

Declaration of Independence, 1776.

Douglass, Frederick. *Life and Times of Frederick Douglass.* Hartford, Conn. Park Publishing Co., 1881.

Goebbels, Joseph. Speech given to an audience of party members at the "Hochschule für Politik," a series of training talks for Nazi Party members, Berlin, January 1928.

Kessler, Ronald. *Inside the White House.* New York: Pocket books, Feb 1st,1995.

Claston A. Bernard

King, Martin Luther, Jr. *Strength to Love.* Minneapolis: Fortress Press, 2010.

Washington, Booker T. *Up from Slavery.* Minoela: Doubleday, 1901.

Woodson, Carter G. *The History of the Negro Church.* Washington, D.C.: Associated Publishers, 1921.

Genesis: Chapter 5:2 (NIV)

62

Printed in Great Britain
by Amazon

74782750R00050